MEDIAEVAL SOURCES
IN TRANSLATION

16

Shyreswood, Peter of Spain, Robert Kilwardby, Raymond Lull, Walter Burleigh, William of Ockham, and Albert of Saxony. The *Isagoge* retained its stature throughout this period since the *Organon* and its imitators remained the basis of logical inquiry. William of Shyreswood's *Introduction to Logic*, for example, presents the predicables in a separate chapter and in Porphyry's order, a practice which was repeated in most authors.

From 1500 to 1850 there is little change in logical theory, though many textbooks were produced. Logic retained a place in the curriculum, but it no longer attracted as much attention as in the past. Formal logic received a sharp attack from Renaissance humanists who belittled Aristotle, scholasticism, and the "presumptions" of philosophers to special knowledge. Throughout all this, however, while some mediaeval logical doctrines pretty much disappeared, such as *suppositio* and *consequentiae*, the predicables and formal logic were taught. The major thrust of the period was discovery, and formal logic was seen as an ordering device, so that nothing new could come of it. For new approaches to logic we need only mention Francis Bacon, Ramus, Jungius, and Arnauld and Nicole of Port Royal. All of these attempts orient logic in a way that does not advance its formalization. Despite the work of Leibnitz in the 17th and 18th centuries, mathematics and logic were disjoined and not to meet again seriously until the 19th century.

The many complex developments of logic until the present cannot be detailed here. The great figures of recent times, men like Boole, Frege, Whitehead, Russell, Carnap, and others produced profound changes in our approach to logic, but logic, like philosophy itself, is seen differently at different times. Perhaps most germane to Porphyry and the controversies which emerged over universals is the recognition that the attempts to incorporate mathematics into logic or the reverse, which stand at the foundation of modern mathematical logic, gave rise to serious questions about the nature and reference of number and about the nature of meaning in general. The style and symbols of the discussion may have changed, but many of the familiar, ancient distinctions were employed again. Frege's *Sinn* and *Bedeutung* are an obvious example. The *Isagoge* presents a limited view of the possibilities of formalization, but many of its problems are also those of contemporary logic.

Isagoge and Metaphysics

Although the attention paid to the *Isagoge* has been due to its connection with the history and development of logic, there is another side to its significance. Logic, even viewed as an organon, was closely connected to metaphysical reasoning, and one should not look upon the *Isagoge* as a simple piece of logical theory since its implications and applications go beyond formal principles of reasoning. The debates over universals were metaphysical, and the Aristotelian distinctions involved in the predicables were applied in the theory of knowledge and first philosophy and theology. To understand this little work, then, one must pay some attention to the relation of the *Isagoge* to metaphysics.

The problem of the reference of general terms undoubtedly arose during the mid-fifth century B.C. together with types of phenomenalism, rhetoric, grammar, theoretical mathematics, and scepticism. Historians of Greek philosophy do not speak of a "problem of universals," and our age succumbs too easily, I think, to viewing the controversy as a mediaeval one. Western philosophy may be fruitfully viewed as a continuing debate over the scope of human understanding, and each major philosopher makes crucial commitments to a theory of human ideation and meaning. The 20th century might be called the Century of Meaning, in which a new term "meaning" replaces an old one, "idea," in order to catch nuances and subtleties that seem obscured by the traditional language.

The problem of universals, or to what do general terms refer, has received varied answers in the past 2500 years, but the responses are usually classified under three terms: realism, conceptualism, and nominalism. The realist asserts the existence of the universal *qua* universal independent of the human mind; the conceptualist asserts that universals *qua* universal exist only in the human mind; and the nominalist that universals do not exist at all, not even in the human mind. As philosophers well know, classifying theorists according to these terms can be difficult and frequently frustrating, but the terminology persists and has its utility.

Up until the 16th century major Western thinkers were realists or conceptualists who wanted to claim knowledge of suprasensible existence in addition to natural knowledge. Nominalists were about but largely rejected and suppressed until the worldly humanism of the great Renaissance led to growing successes in the knowledge of the natural world. The generally nominalist response of modern philosophers after Francis Bacon was based on the conviction that natural knowledge did not imply realism, and probably not conceptualism, both of which were buttresses of a repressive theological-political system that attempted to control inquiry. Since the object of natural knowledge was a nature open to the immediate scrutiny of the senses and reasoning powers, there was no recognized need to posit an analogue to the Greek νοῦς and Latin *intellectus* that mysteriously grasped immaterial natures. With astronomy and physics leading the way, somewhat parallel to the 6th and 5th centuries B.C., philosophers attempted to found a sound epistemology and metaphysics of natural knowledge and either reject suprasensible reality or set it aside in its own realm where it could not contaminate the natural philosopher. An empirical sensationalism, a denial of a strong sense of *intellectus* or νοῦς, a substitution of hypothesis and probability for certitude, the emergence of time rather than eternity as the criterion of the real, and the adoption of a linear model of the world for a spherical one, led to a gradual transformation of Western thinking whose consequences are still being worked out. The development of these notions is not uniform, of course, but their course is clearly marked.

The change in metaphor is crucial for the history of metaphysics and logic, and so for the understanding of Porphyry's *Isagoge*. Metaphysics from Plato on had shown two opposite tendencies, to see reality (1) as temporal and so in a linear series, as Protagoras and the radical phenomenalism of τὸ πᾶν κίνησις ἦν in the *Theaetetus* (156a5), and (2) as eternal or non-temporal, in some ultimate way, and so complete and summed up like a sphere or circle. One might state the issue in this way: if existence is linear, the only point of reference for knowledge is the past by an accumulation of discrete data. A human mind may accumulate during its lifetime bits of information about preceding events in the series and by observing similarities and differences hypothesize that coming events will accord with developed rules. Reference, then, is limited to the past. If existence is spherical, it is at all times summed up or totaled. Any segment of the temporal line can be referred to the Whole and understood. Instead of a linear series one has a set of whole-part relations. Implicit in the time-series is a pattern or λόγος that expresses the eternal in time at a given moment. Some doctrine of participation or analogy must account for the relation between the partiality of time and the wholeness of eter-

nity. The whole must be immanent in the parts or else there are
no parts, only independent segments. The eternal metaphysical
scheme dominated Western thinking until the 16th century when
serious changes came about, coming to full flower in the 19th
century, a process which George Boas has called the "Ac-
ceptance of Time."[8] Aristotle's logic, treated as a class logic,
rests on the spherical metaphor of whole and part. The Tree of
Porphyry provides a striking example. In the *Isagoge* the three
terms "individual," "singular," and "particular," reflect different approaches to space-time objects, and an adequate grasp
of these nuances of metaphor is necessary for a firm grasp of the
issues as seen by the ancients. There are several notes to the
translation which attempt to clarify these distinctions.

Porphyry's introduction, then, is important to us as a
document in the history of metaphysics and the theory of
knowledge, and perhaps more so than as a logical one. Its influence is due to the logical tradition of Aristotle's *Organon*, but
its significance lies in the connection of that tradition to
metaphysical and epistemological issues.

Commentaries of Boethius

These two commentaries merit special, though brief, mention
because of their influence. Evidence indicates that besides the
Greek commentary of Ammonius (d. 480) other commentaries
on the *Isagoge* had preceded. It is thought that Boethius in his
own work used Ammonius or Ammonius' source. The first commentary is less well known, shorter (2 books), written in the

---

[8] *Dominant Themes of Modern Philosophy*, George Boas, The Ronald Press Co., New
York, 1957, p. 612.

form of a colloquy between Boethius as teacher and Fabius as student. The structure is patterned after Porphyry's own extant commentary on the *Categories, Expositio Per Interrogationem et Responsionem*, CAG IV. Although Boethius uses the translation of Victorinus as the basis of his work, he paraphrases and sometimes corrects his predecessor's version. The second commentary is a straightforward analysis of Porphyry in five books based on Boethius' own translation.

Of some importance in the second work is Boethius' attempt at a solution to the problems posed as the deeper questions in the opening section of the *Isagoge*. Boethius professes to follow Alexander of Aphrodisias; and, as is generally agreed, the solution is more a statement of an Aristotelian position than anything else, since grave questions remain untouched. Boethius asserts that the mind collects a *similitudo* or likeness ("A likeness is nothing else but a kind of unity of quality." E.S. p. 228, 20) from singular things and thinks a universal. Thus, generic and specific contents "subsist in connection with sensible things but are understood without bodies." E.S. p. 166, 22-23. What is involved epistemologically and metaphysically in collection is untreated. There is no reason to regard this solution as that of Boethius since he consciously follows a Peripatetic line of argument and the commentary treats of an introduction to Aristotle: "therefore, we have followed Aristotle's opinion quite carefully, not because we approved of it especially, but because our book is written with Aristotle's book in mind, his *Praedicamenta (Categories)*." E.S. p. 167, 17-20. In the first commentary Boethius had asserted the existence of the predicables and predicaments "which are put into things and in some way are united with them" otherwise there would be no point in discussing them. He did not, however, introduce the notions of *similitudo* and collection. Also, in the second commentary a Platonic view of the predicables occasionally emerges, i.e., "therefore, species also subsist before individuals." P. 316, 22-23. Both commentaries can be consulted with profit, especially the introductory portions, although the later sections can be helpful in lesser problems of interpretation.

Text and Translation

In making this translation I have used the following main sources:

Porphyry's Greek Text:

> *Porphyrii Isagoge et in Aristotelis Categorias Commentarium,* ed. A. Busse, CAG, Vol. IV (1), 1887.

Latin Translations:

> *Porphyrii Introductio in Aristotelis Categorias a Boethio Translata,* ed. A. Busse, CAG, Vol. IV (1), 1887.
>
> *Porphyrii Isagoge, Translatio Boethii, Aristoteles Latinus,* 1 6-7, ed. L. Minio-Paluello, ad. B. G. Dod, Bruges-Paris, Desclée de Brouwer, 1966.
>
> "L'Isagoge Latine de Marius Victorinus," Paul Monceaux, pp. 291-310, *Philologie et Linguistique,* Mélanges offerts à Louis Havet, Paris, Hachette, 1909.
>
> *Isagoges Fragmenta M. Victorino Interprete, Aristoteles Latinus,* 1 6-7, ed. L. Minio-Paluello, ad. B. G. Dod, Bruges-Paris, Desclée de Brouwer, 1966.
>
> *Porphyrii Introductio, Julio Pacio interprete,* pp. 7-26, *Aristotelis Opera Omnia,* quae extant brevi paraphrasi et litterae perpetuo inhaerente expositione illustrata a Silvestro Mauro, S.J., 1658, repub. by F. Ehrle, S.J., Parisiis, 1885.

French Translation:

> *Isagoge*, par J. Tricot, Librairie Philosophique, J. Vrin, Paris, 1947.

Greek Commentaries:

> *Ammonii in Porphyrii Isagogen sive V voces*, ed. A. Busse, CAG, Vol. IV (3), Berlin, 1891.
>
> *Eliae (olim David) in Porphyrii Isagogen et Aristotelis Commentaria*, ed. A. Busse, CAG, Vol. XVIII (1), Berlin, 1900.
>
> *Davidis Prolegomena et in Porphyrii Isagogen Commentarium*, ed. A. Busse, CAG, Vol. XVIII (2), Berlin, 1904.

Latin Commentaries:

> *In Isagogen Porphyrii Commenta, Anicii Manlii Severini Boethii*, CSEL, Vol. 48, Operum Pars I, Georgius Schepss, Vindobonae, 1906.
>
> *Analyticus Commentarius, Iuli Pacii a Beriga, In Porphyrii Isagogen et Aristotelis Organum*, Aureliae Allobrogum, 1605.
>
> *Aristotelis Opera Omnia*, quae extant brevi paraphrasi et litterae perpetuo inhaerente expositione illustrata a Silvestro Mauro, S.J., 1658.

Busse's Greek text of Porphyry in CAG is usable, though it is clear that a better text could be produced. The best text of Boethius' excellent translation is in *Aristoteles Latinus* though my initial work was done many years ago with the CAG, in which there are misprints and doubtful readings. The Latin translation of Marius Victorinus, most accurately presented in *Aristoteles Latinus*, was reconstructed by Paul Monceaux and is worth examining, for it is the oldest version of Porphyry that we possess. Victorinus must be used with some caution since "C'est moins une traduction qu'une adaptation."[9] Pacius' version is valuable for the change in philosophical terminology during the intervening 1000 years, yet perhaps what is most significant is the continuity of expression over such a long period of time rather than the change. The three Greek and three Latin commentaries were supplemented by samplings from Alcuin, Abelard, John of Salisbury, Duns Scotus, and William of Ockham. There is a large number of Latin commentaries on the predicables in mediaeval logical works. It is doubtful that consulting additional sources would improve the translation, and additional notes would seem unjustified for this short work. As it is, John of Salisbury might well disapprove of the detail already evident.

[9] "L' Isagoge Latine de Marius Victorinus," P. Monceaux, *Philologie et Linguistique*, Mélanges offerts à Louis Havet, Paris, Hachette, 1909, p. 395.

Conventions

Spec*ies* when so printed indicates the plural.

[] are used for the transliteration of Greek words.

() are used for brackets which occur in Busse's text in CAG.

Letters ([a]) are used to indicate, primarily, readings in Boethius which differ from Porphyry's text.

AL stands for *Aristoteles Latinus*.

ALG stands for *Aristoteles Latinus*, Greek apparatus.

B stands for Boethius. All Boethian translations of the *Isagoge* are from the text printed in AL.

CAG *Commentaria in Aristotelem Graeca.*

CSEL *Corpus Scriptorum Ecclesiasticorum Latinorum.*

E.P. *Editionis Primae Commenta Boethii.*

E.S. *Editionis Secundae Commenta Boethii.*

Is stands for the Greek text of the *Isagoge* in CAG.

P stands for Pacius.

V stands for Victorinus.

Footnote references have been simplified where there is no ambiguity.

For textual differences between Porphyry and Boethius consult *Aristoteles Latinus*, although I have indicated a few which may be of immediate interest. The marginal pagination indicates approximately parallel lines in the Greek text.

introduction to genus, species, etc

THE *ISAGOGE* OF PORPHYRY, THE PHOENICIAN, THE PUPIL OF PLOTINUS OF LYCOPOLIS

To understand Aristotle's categories, Chrysaorius, one must know the nature of genus, difference, species, property, and ac- 5
cident. This knowledge is also useful for giving definitions and generally for division and demonstration.[10] I shall make for you a concise review of this traditional teaching as befits an in-troduction and try to recount what our predecessors said. I shall avoid the deeper issues and in a few words try to explain the simpler notions. For example, I shall put aside the investigation of certain profound questions concerning genera and spec*ies*, 10
since such an undertaking requires more detailed examination:
(1) whether genera or spec*ies* exist in themselves[11] or reside in mere concepts alone;[a] (2) whether, if they exist, they are cor-

---

[a] ἐν μόναις ψιλαῖς ἐπινοίαις κεῖται ... B: *in solis nudis purisque intellectibus posita sunt.*

[10] Διαίρεσις or division is a technique developed by Plato particularly in the *Sophist* and *Statesman.* Ἀπόδειξις or demonstration is the Aristotelian method of proof, involving the syllogism. which yields scientific knowledge. *Posterior Analytics,* I, 2, 71b 17-19.
[11] Following Tricot. Ὑφίστασθαι becomes a strong word in neoplatonism and frequent-ly denotes what "really" exists. The familiar transliteration "hypostasis" for ὑπόστασις in Plotinus is designed to avoid circumlocutions such as "fundamentally real." In his trans-lation the terms are rendered by "exist." Boethius uses the appropriate form of *subsisto.* but the English "subsist" confuses more philosophers than it helps. The distinction be-tween subsist and exist becomes important in neoplatonism where subsist is the chief reality word. Space-time objects exist but always under the shadow of appearance. The same distinction in the hands of an empiricist alters the force of the terms, so that subsist becomes ephemeral and abstract while exist becomes the reality term. For Boethius' translation of some key Greek philosophical terms see *Contra Eutychen.* III.

28   ISAGOGE

poreal or incorporeal; and (3) whether they exist apart or in
sense objects and in dependence on them.[12] Instead, I shall try
15 to make clear to you how in logic ᵇ the ancients, and especially
the Peripatetics, dealt with genus, difference, and the rest.[13]

GENUS

Neither genus nor species appears to have one sense, for
genus can mean (1) a collection of things related to one another
20 because each is related to some one thing in a particular way. In
this sense the Heraclids[14] are said to be a family [*genos*] because
of the relationship of descent from one man, Heracles. The
many people related to each other because of this kinship

ᵇ λογικώτερον B: *probabiliter.*

---

[12] Porphyry's text for this third question is πότερον χωριστὰ ἢ ἐν τοῖς αἰσθητοῖς καὶ περὶ
ταῦτα ὑφεστῶτα B: *utrum separata a sensibilibus an in sensibilibus posita et circa ea con-
stantia.* ... V: *utrum separata an ipsis sensibilibus juncta.* P: *utrum separata sint, an in
rebus sensibilibus et circa has consistant.* Elias comments, χωριστὰ τὰ πρὸ τῶν πολλῶν
νοητέον, ἐν τοῖς αἰσθητοῖς τὰ ἐν τοῖς πολλοῖς, περὶ ταῦτα ὑφεστῶτα τὰ ἐπὶ τοῖς πολλοῖς, ...
p. 49, 22-23.

[13] Porphyry intends to avoid metaphysical issues and to confine his attention to logical
considerations. Logic was not considered a part of philosophy but a preparation for the
more difficult inquiries into physics, ethics, and theology or metaphysics. According to
Ammonius, pp. 43-45, philosophical knowledge is built on categorical propositions
which are true or false. These propositions have subjects and predicates, and it is the job
of logic to determine what things are subjects and what are predicates. A metaphysical or
physical inquiry would pass beyond an introduction and involve the profound questions
that Porphyry chooses to avoid. Later, p. 69, Ammonius calls Porphyry's inquiry conceptual, ἐννοηματικός. Porphyry himself says in his commentary on the *Categories* that
the *Categories* "concern sounds indicative of things," περὶ φωνῶν σημαντικῶν τῶν
πραγμάτων, p. 57, 6. See A. C. Lloyd's "Neoplatonic Logic and Aristotelian Logic —
II," *Phronesis* 1, 2, pp. 151-152. For Boethius' understanding of λογικώτερον see E.S.
12, pp. 168-169.

[14] This example also appears in *Plotini Opera,* VI, 1, 3, ed. Henry et Schwyzer, 3
vols., Desclée de Brouwer, Paris, 1951-1973.

deriving from Heracles are called the family of the Heraclids since they as a family are separate from other families.

In another sense (2) genus means the source[15] of each man's birth, whether from his father or from the place in which he was born. When we say that Orestes has his descent [genos] from Tantalus, Hyllus from Heracles, and again that Pindar is of Theban stock [genos], Plato of Athenian, we use the term in this sense. In fact each man's fatherland, in a way, is a source of his birth, just as his father is. This meaning seems to be obvious, for those who descend from the family of Heracles are called Heraclids, those from Cecrops and their kinsmen Cecropids.[16]

So far the source of each man's birth has been called a genus, and also the many people who spring from one source, as Heracles, since, by distinguishing and separating this group of men from the rest, we said that the whole collection of Heraclids was a family. In another sense (3) genus means that to which the species is subordinate, a meaning asserted as a definition of genus, perhaps, because of a similarity of this sense with the two former senses. For such a genus is a source, in a way, of the species under itself and it seems also to contain the whole subordinate multitude.

Genus, then, has three senses, but discussion among philosophers concerns the third. Philosophers explain[17] genus as

P. 2

5

10

15

---

[15] Ἀρχή. A technical philosophical term usually translated as "principle." This English term does not include the range of the Greek since Heracles is a source but not a principle. "Foundation" seems a close synonym in many contexts. The Greek idea is that of a beginning, a source of generation, hence foundation and ground. Throughout this translation "source" is used. Boethius uses *principium*.

[16] All Athenians are Cecropids, descendants of Cecrops, the mythical first king of Athens. Usually Boethius substitutes Roman persons and gods as he does in his other works. Pacius reproduces the Greek examples.

[17] ὃ καὶ ὑπογράφοντες ἀποδεδώκασι γένος εἶναι λέγοντες κτλ. The Greek commentators point out that the predicables can only be sketched out and shown, not defined in the

pre dict ded

that predicated essentially of many things which differ in species, as animal, for example.[18] For some predications are said of only one thing, as individual terms[19] like "Socrates," "this"

strict sense by giving the species and genus. Genus has no genus. Duns Scotus, on the other hand, holds that the predicables can be defined, not merely described. *Super Universalia Porphyrii*, Ioannis Duns Scoti, Opera Omnia, Vol. I, Lugduni, MDCXXXIX (p. 98, Q. 15, 3). The general problem of the relation of a symbol system to itself has continued to exercise logicians. Tricot, p. 14, n. 4, says "le verbe ὑπογράφειν a le sens *definire*, et ἀποδιδόναι, enarrare." *Isagoge*, French translation, J. Tricot, Librairie Philosophique, J. Vrin, Paris, 1947. The reverse seems true. Is: ὑπογράφοντες B: *describentes*, Is: ἀποδεδώκασι B: *adsignaverunt*. Boethius remarks, "Carefully he says *describentes*, not *definientes*; for a definition arises from a genus, but a genus can not have another genus." E.S. p. 180, 20-22. A *descriptio* is given, not a *definitio*. "A *descriptio*, as we said in an earlier book, is a kind of sketch of a thing based on its qualities and like a characterization from outward appearances. For, when many qualities unite together so that all of them at the same time are equal to the thing to which they apply — this is called a *descriptio*, unless this collection is composed of a genus or differences." E.S. p. 181, 8-13. V: *quod definientes ita declarant* P: *Quod etiam descriptione explicarunt*.

[18] This definition is taken verbatim from *Topics* 102a 31-32. Several terms deserve comment: (1) *Predicated* In most cases "is predicated" translates κατηγορεῖται, an Aristotelian technical term which can be transliterated to "is categorized." Aristotle apparently is the first to employ κατηγορεῖσθαι in this technical sense. In the language of later logicians all terms are categorematic, indicating substance, quantity, qualification, relation, and so on, or are syncategorematic, logical constants joining the categoric terms together, such as "and," "or," "but," and so on. All categorematic terms used in propositions will be usages in one of the 10 categories, the possible ways in which language can refer to or characterize the things of the world. Another commonly used term is λέγεται, literally meaning "is said of." Λέγεται and κατηγορεῖται are frequently used synonymously. Occasionally for λέγεται "is said of" is better since it is vaguer and leaves indeterminate whether words or things are under discussion. (2) *Essentially* More verbosely "in the category of essence." "... for, of the common predicates, that which falls most definitely in the category of essence (ἐν τῷ τί ἐστι) must be the genus." *Topics*, 108b 22-23, E. S. Forster. Boethius and Victorinus render ἐν τῷ τί ἐστι as *in eo quod quid sit*. (3) *Many things* There is no genus with one species. See n. 32. Also *Topics*, 123a 30.

[19] There are three terms used in the text for individuals and particulars: ἄτομον, ἕκαστον, and κατὰ μέρος. By far the most frequent is ἄτομον, uncuttable. Ἄτομον is translated by "individual," τὸ καθ' ἕκαστον "singular," and τὸ κατὰ μέρος "particular." Boethius translates *individuum, singulare*, and *particulare*. "Individual" refers to the undivided or indivisible and is usually applied to space-time objects, but the metaphor would allow the term to be applied to God who is both undivided and indivisible. Aristotle, for example, at times uses ἄτομον to mean the lowest species. Ἄτομον indicates

man, and "this" object;[20] but others are said of many things, such as genera, species, differences, properties, and accidents that occur jointly in many and not uniquely in some one thing.[21] An example of genus is "animal"; of species, "man"; of difference, "rational"; of property, "capable of laughing"; of accident, "white," "black," and "sitting."[22]

Genera, therefore, differ from those terms which are predicated of only one thing because they are explained as being predicated of many things. They differ from species which are predicated of many things. Although species are predicated of many things, the many do not differ in species but in number.

20

25

that the integrity and wholeness of the object lies in its cohesiveness but does not necessarily make clear the kind of whole referred to. In its reference to the space-time individual it indicates what can no longer be divided in existence without its destruction. "Singular" involves a linear metaphor of things set side by side, one after another, each having independent existence. "Particular," on the other hand, connotes the smallest part or division of the circle of being which has independent existence. See n. 32. David's account is somewhat different, and he does not discuss κατὰ μέρος. Τὸ καθ' ἕκαστον is used, he says, "since each of them can be comprehended (lit. be taken aside) by itself" (p. 97, 27-28). Although an individual is cut or divided into hands, feet, and a head, yet its parts are only parts and are not complete in themselves. The individual, then, is the last complete entity in the chain of being. For the use of the word "term" see n. 22.

[20] Τῶν γὰρ κατηγορουμένων τὰ μὲν καθ' ἑνὸς λέγεται μόνου, ὡς τὰ ἄτομα οἶον Σωκράτης καὶ τὸ οὖτος καὶ τὸ τοῦτο ... "Predications" is an inadequate translation of τῶν κατηγορουμένων. "Socrates" and "this" are not predicates but names of subjects; nonetheless, they do occur "in the category of" substance as referring to primary substances, existing particular things. Categorematic terms name things and their characteristics, and all words "speak about," λέγειν, the world.

[21] Two kinds of accident are involved: (1) τὰ συμβεβηκότα κοινῶς, common accidents, which occur in several different particulars, as black and white; and (2) τὰ συμβεβηκότα ἰδίως, those particular accidents which actually belong to a particular, as this white in this body. Boethius translates accidentia communiter sed non proprie alicui, AL, p. 7, 5.

[22] Porphyry thinks of the five predicables as classifications of terms, and in one expression he makes this quite clear, τὸ οὖτος (Is 2, 18). See also, Is 3, 15; 7, 19. As Porphyry said in the beginning he wishes to avoid the profound questions, especially the exact kind of reference which the terms in the 10 categories possess. Generally I have not used quotation marks in this translation, preferring the ambiguity to an overinterpretation of the text. Sometimes, too, Porphyry uses the generic article (LS and J, B, I, 2) rather than a specifying article (Ibid., B, I, 5).

For example, man, as species, is predicated of Socrates and
Plato, who do not differ from one another in species but in number; but animal, a genus, is predicated of man, ox, and horse,

P. 3 which differ from one another in species as well as in number. In
turn genus differs from property because property is predicated
of only the one species to which it belongs and of individuals
under the species,[c] as capable of laughing is predicated of man
only and of particular men, but the genus is predicated not of

5 one but of many different spec*ies*.[d]

Genus also differs from difference and from common accidents.[21] Although differences and common accidents are
predicated of many things differing in species, they are not
predicated essentially.[e] If we ask how the differences and common accidents are predicated, we assert that they are predicated

10 qualitatively, not essentially. For to the question "What sort of
thing is man?" we reply, "Rational"; and to the question
"What sort of thing is a crow?" we reply, "Black." Rational is
a difference, black an accident. When, however, we are asked
what man is, we answer, "Animal." Animal is the genus of
man.[23]

---

[c] B: *sub una specie.*
[d] ALG correctly.
[e] B adds *sed in eo quod quale quid sit.* Retained in ALG but doubted by Busse.

---

[23] The doctrine in this passage separates the specific difference *qua* quality from the
essence. Porphyry is following the thrust of the discussion in *Topics* 128a 20-29 where
Aristotle asserts that the genus most appropriately indicates essence. Also *Metaphysics*
1024b 5-6. At *Topics* 122b 16-18 he asserts "... no differentia indicates the essence, but
rather some quality, such as 'pedestrian' and 'biped' " (Loeb). To indicate the essence of
the species one names the genus. To indicate the essence of a primary substance one
names the species and *a fortiori* the difference. *Categories* 2b 7-22. For Aristotle see the
brief but important observations of E. de Strycker in G. E. L. Owen, *Aristotle on Dialectic: The Topics*, Clarendon Press, Oxford, 1968, pp. 154-155. Later in Porphyry's
discussion of difference, pp. 42-47 of the translation, he distinguishes three kinds, one of

predicated of
"spoken of"

We conclude, then, that (1) the genus, since it is predicated of
many things, differs from individual terms which are predicated   15
of only one thing; (2) since the genus is a genus of things which
differ in species, it differs from terms predicated as spec*ies* or as
properties; and (3) since it is predicated essentially, it is separate
from differences and common accidents, each of which is
predicated ᶠ not essentially but qualitatively or as some degree of
quality.²⁴

Our present sketch of the notion of genus is sufficient.   20

ᶠ B adds *de his de quibus praedicantur.*

which is specific difference which brings about the divisions of genera into species. Thus,
two kinds of difference are qualitative and accidental, and the third is specific and essential. At the conclusion of a discussion of this distinction Ammonius remarks, "Consequently, the genus is analogous to matter, the differences to form. Since matter provides
existence for each thing while the form provides qualitative difference, it is reasonable for
the genus to be predicated essentially, analogous to matter, and for difference to be
predicated qualitatively, analogous to form." P. 107, 17-21. According to Elias, in
definitions differences do not remain differences, but when taken together with genera
become spec*ies* (p. 56, 30 — p. 57, 11). "Every form is a quality, so with good reason
every difference is called a quality." E.S., p. 269, 3-4. Scotus marks the difference in use,
Q. XIX, p. 105. Consult A. C. Lloyd's "Neoplatonic Logic and Aristotelian Logic."

²⁴ Although Porphyry's explanation of the predicables is mostly in Aristotelian terms,
his use of πῶς ἔχον (probably πὼς ἔχον) is Stoic. Plotinus at VI, 1, 25, 2-3 lists the Stoic
categories as ὑποκείμενα καὶ ποιὰ καὶ πὼς ἔχοντα καὶ πρός τί πως ἔχοντα, or subject,
quality, disposition, and relative disposition. Dispositions are modes of qualities: καὶ ἔτι
τὰ μὲν ποιὰ περὶ τὴν ὕλην πως ἔχοντα, τὰ ἰδίως δέ πως ἔχοντα περὶ τὰ ποιά (Plotinus, VI,
1, 30, 5-7). Plotinus is perplexed by the Stoic attempt to incorporate into the one
category of πὼς ἔχον a host of Aristotelian categories, such as quantity, time, place, and
so on. He remarks that πὼς ἔχον comes closest to the Aristotelian κεῖσθαι and ἔχειν, state
and possession. "Size, colour, place, time, action, passion, possession, motion, state, in
short all the Aristotelian categories, with the exception of substance, whenever they apply
to an object independently of its relation to other objects, belong to the category of
variety (πὼς ἔχον)." E. Zeller, *The Stoics, Epicureans, and Sceptics*, trans. by O. J.
Reichel, repr. N.Y., Russell and Russell, Inc., 1962, p. 107. Porphyry seems consistently
to use this expression in a broad sense except at Is 17, 12 where it seems to correspond
directly to the Aristotelian category of state or posture, κεῖσθαι. Ammonius treats πὼς ἔχον
as equivalent to τὸ συμβεβηκός, accident. For example, p. 64, 22; p. 95, 2. See Boethius

SPECIES

Although species [*eidos*] is used (1) to designate the shapeliness of an individual, as it has been said,[25]

P. 4   First a beauty [*eidos*] worthy of absolute power, species is also said to be (2) that under the defined genus. We customarily say, then, that man is a species of animal, since animal is its genus; white a species of color; triangle a species of

5   figure. In defining genus we mentioned the species by saying that the genus is that predicated essentially of many things which differ in species. If we now say that the species is that under the defined genus, we ought to realize that we must define one in terms of the other since the genus is a genus of something and the species is a species of something.

Our philosophic predecessors, therefore, especially the

10   Peripatetics,[26] define the species as (3a) what is ordered under

---

as well, E.S. pp. 265-266, 317. Elias comments, "Accident is two-fold, separable or inseparable. Being predicated qualitatively is proper for an inseparable accident, but being predicated as disposition is proper for a separable one. For example, how is Socrates disposed? He is healthy or ill, which are separable accidents" (p. 60, 16-19). Boethius regularly uses a form of *se habens* plus an adverb such as *quomodo*. Pacius in the first three occurrences uses a variant of *quomodo quid affectum est*; in the last three he closely parallels Boethius. Πῶς ἔχον occurs six times in the *Isagoge*. No English translation seems to fit uniformly, so each occurrence of the term is noted. For a recent discussion and bibliography see J. M. Rist, *Stoic Philosophy*, Cambridge U. Press, 1969, pp. 167-172. Also, Trendelenburg's *Geschichte der Kategorienlehre*, Georg Olms, Hildesheim, 1963 (repr. from 1846), pp. 227-231.

[25] Euripides, *Aeolus*, 15, 2, Nauck, *Tragicorum Graecorum Fragmenta*, adiecit B. Snell, Olms, Hildesheim, 1964, p. 367.

Here εἶδος means the beauty of physical form and manliness. V: "For the form of each man is called the species, but form also means the beauty of one's appearance. So, those who are quite handsome we call *speciosus*." Maurus comments, "... we say 'species' from *spectare* (looking), and so it primarily means visible form or exterior appearance. Because of this meaning *speciosus* means the same as *formosus*, and species means the same as *formositas* or *pulchritudo*" (p. 9, 1).

[26] An interpretation of the vague ἀποδιδόασιν based on the concluding lines of the introduction, and elsewhere in the same way.

the genus and what the genus is predicated of essentially. They
say also (3b) that species is that predicated essentially of many
things which differ in number.[27] This last definition, however,
will define the lowest species,[28] viz. what is a species only, but
the former definitions will apply as well to those classes[29] which
are not the lowest species.
What is meant will be clear from the following. In each   15
category there are the highest classes,[28] the lowest classes, and
some which are between the highest and the lowest. There is a
highest genus beyond which there can be no other superior
genus; there is a lowest species after which there can be no
subordinate species; and between the highest genus and the
lowest species there are some classes which are genera and
species at the same time, since they are comprehended in
relation to the highest genus and to the lowest species.   20
Let us make the meaning clear with reference to one
category.[30] Substance[31] is itself a genus; under this is body; and

---

[27] See *The Logic of William of Ockham*, E. A. Moody, p. 72 ff.

[28] Εἰδικώτατον B: *specialissimum*, γενικώτατον B: *generalissimum*. Tricot points out,
p. 18, that these terms are not found in Aristotle. Bonitz, *Index Aristotelicus*, lists the
simple adjective γενικός in *Topics* 101b 18 and 102a 36.

[29] The Greek is εἴδη, species. In the next few pages this term is used many times to ex-
press the notion of class relation. In the *Topics* Aristotle uses εἶδος for his class relations,
reserving ἰδέα for Plato's forms. "... the categories ... are only fixed classes of things
arranged in this order so that species are subordinate to genera, individuals to species,
..." Pacius, *Analyticus Commentarius*, p. 5.

[30] Now follows the famous Tree of Porphyry. See Kneale, p. 232. The method of
definition by genus and differentia implies such a tree, whose antecedents can be found in
Plato's method of division and Aristotle's *Topics*, 143 ff., for example. The notion of a
tree is suggested in E.P. by the expression "... all the unity of higher genera will be
divided into various branching species" (p. 78, 10-11).

[31] Οὐσία. Aristotle's term for the fundamental category. The word is an abstract noun
made from the present participle feminine οὖσα of the verb "to be," εἶναι. It is traditional
to translate οὐσία as substance even though its connection with "to be" is obscured and,
so, its relation to Plato's and Parmenides' doctrines and to Aristotle's own views about
being, τὸ ὄν. All things considered there appears to be no suitable English alternative, in-

under body animate body, under which is animal; under animal
is rational animal, under which is man; under man are Socrates,
25   Plato, and particular men. Of these substance is the highest
genus, and it is a genus only, while man is the lowest species,
and it is a species only. Body is a species of substance but a
genus of animate body. Animate body is a species of body but a
genus of animal. Animal is a species of animate body, but a
30   genus of rational animal. Rational animal is a species of animal,
but a genus of man. Man is a species of rational animal, but it is
not also a genus of particular men. It is a species only. Every
species which is predicated immediately[g] prior to individuals
P. 5   will be a species only, never a genus. Just as, then, substance is
highest because there is nothing superior to itself and is the
highest genus, so too man is a species after which there is no
species[h] nor anything able to be divided into spec*ies*.[i] Of individuals (Socrates, Plato, and "this white"[j] are individuals)
5   there can be only a species, namely the last species and, as we
said, the lowest species. The intermediate classes will be spec*ies*
of prior classes but genera of posterior classes.

ᵏ προσεχῶς κατηγορούμενον B: *quod proximum est.*
ʰ οὐκ ἔστιν εἶδος B: *alia inferior species.*
ⁱ εἰς εἴδη B omits.
ʲ B omits.

---

cluding Owens' "entity." See Joseph Owens, *The Doctrine of Being in the Aristotelian
'Metaphysics,'* Pontifical Institute of Mediaeval Studies, Toronto, 2nd ed. revised, 1963,
pp. 137-154. Aristotle's own definition of substance is as follows: "A *substance* — that
which is called a substance most strictly, primarily, and most of all — is that which is
neither said of a subject nor in a subject, e.g., the individual man or the individual horse.
The species in which the things primarily called substances are, are called *secondary substances*, as also are the genera of these species. For example, the individual man belongs
in a species, man, and animal is a genus of the species; so these — both man and
animal — are called secondary substances." *Aristotle's Categories and De Interpretatione*,
J. L. Ackrill, pp. 5-6, *Categories*, 2a 11-18.

It follows that these intermediates have two relations: one with prior classes in which they are called spe*cies* and the other with posterior classes in which they are called genera. The extremities have one relation. The highest genus is related to the 10 classes under itself,[k] since it is the highest genus of all, but it has no relation at all with prior classes, since it is the highest, like a primary source,[l] and, as we said, that beyond which there can be no superior genus.[m] The lowest species, too, has one relation, that with its prior classes. It has no sort of class relation with its posteriors, although it is called a species of individuals. The 15 lowest species, however, is called (1) a species of individuals because[n] it contains[32] them but (2) a species of prior classes because it is contained by them.

They, therefore, define the highest genus as a genus which is not a species, and again, that beyond which there can be no superior genus; but they define the lowest species as a species (1) which is not a genus, (2) which can not be divided further 20

---

[k] τὰ ὑφ' ἑαυτό B: *quae posteriora sunt.*
[l] ἀνωτάτω ὄν καί ὡς πρώτη ἀρχή B: *cum sit supremum et primum principium.*
[m] B omits all after ἀρχή.
[n] B interprets ὡς περιέχον αὐτά as *velut ea continens.*

---

[32] Περιέχον, which appeared earlier at Is 2, 13. Literally, to hold around on all sides. In the preceding sentence Porphyry denied any class relation (class to class) between the lowest species and the particulars. Now he points out that between the lowest species and its members there is a legitimate relation, that of περιέχον, a term applied as well to the relation of classes to each other. Most modern philosophers, I think, would say that the use of the same term obscures the great difference between these two relations, class to particular and class to class (see Is 8, 1-3); on the other hand, Porphyry saw a similarity in the two relations, that of inclusion and limitation. The way in which the inclusions and limitations function, however, seems quite different. (Ammonius recognized that there was a difference but did not discuss it in detail. P. 80, 9-12.) The relation of higher to lower classes can be conceived of as a series of concentric circles, the larger circle (class) enclosing the smaller (class). Analogously the lowest species encloses the particulars,

into spec*ies*, and (3) which is predicated essentially of many things differing in number. The spec*ies* intermediate between the extremes they call subordinate genera and spec*ies*, and they regard each of them as a species and a genus, since each is comprehended in relation to the highest genus and the lowest

P. 6   species. The spec*ies* prior to the lowest spec*ies* which rise up to the highest genus are called both genera° and spec*ies*, as well as subordinate genera, as Agamemnon, son of Atreus, descendant of Pelops, descendant of Tantalus, and finally descendant of Zeus. Genealogies, however, usually lead up to one member, say

---

° Tricot omits γένη τε.

---

trying to encompass what is essentially indefinite and without limits, the number of individuals. The lowest species is the smallest scientifically significant limitation that can be applied to existence, since the particular substance is the only independent being in space and time. "... what, because of its incomprehensible multiplicity, could not be brought under systematic study, by the small number of genera ... might become subject to the mind and to knowledge." E.S. p. 143, 17-20. On this theory class or species relations are unchanging and, therefore, eternally fixed. Depending on one's metaphysics such relations are among smaller or larger bits of being, concepts, or ranges of symbolic use. Relations between particular existing things and their classes change since the particular beings come into being and pass away. Both time and space are involved with particulars; neither is of concern to the classes. The closeness to and dependency of time and space on the unchanging is part of the pervasive metaphysics of antiquity. For Porphyry, persuaded by Plotinus and by Platonism, the great sphere of being stretches from circumference to center like a series of concentric circles which become smaller and smaller and finally, crossing the time-space line, are pluralized into many circles belonging to various types. For philosophers who regard time and space as defective kinds of existence and for whom eternity and immateriality are existence *par excellence* this use of περιέχειν seems natural. Did not the *Timaeus* (36d-e) assert that body is within the immaterial soul? The wisdom of such a use is questioned when a philosopher regards the particulars as primary existents and the status of species and classes as problematic. If the classes are but symbolic uses invented by man for his convenience, then one can not safely use περιέχειν in this context. For Aristotle's use of περιέχειν for class inclusion see *Topics* 144b 12-30 and F. Solmsen's "Dialectic Without Forms," in G. E. L. Owen, p. 64. Solmsen also notes Plato's use at *Sophist* 250b 8.

for example Zeus, the source.ᵖ But in genera and species this is 5
not the case, for being³³ is not one common genus of all things,
nor are all things of the same genus because of one highest
genus, as Aristotle says.³⁴

But let us lay down, as Aristotle does in the *Categories*, ten
primary genera as ten primary sources. If, then, anyone names
all things beings, he will name them homonymously, he says,
but not synonymously; for if being³³ were one common genus of
all things, all things would be called beings synonymously.³⁵ 10
There is a community of being, however, among the ten primary
genera in name only, none at all according to the definition of
the word. There are, therefore, ten highest genera, while the
lowest species are indefinite in number, yet not infinite. Individuals, which are posterior to the lowest species, are in-
finite.³⁶ It is for this reason that Plato kept urging us to descend

---

ᵖ ἀλλ᾽ ἐπὶ μὲν τῶν γενεαλογιῶν εἰς ἕνα ἀνάγουσι, φέρε εἰπεῖν τὸν Δία, τὴν ἀρχὴν ὡς ἐπὶ
τὸ πλεῖστον B: *sed in familiis quidem plerumque ad unum reducuntur principium, verbi
gratia ad Jovem.*

---

³³ *Τὸ ὄν.* The present participle neuter of the verb "to be." Boethius translates *ens,* for
ὄντα, *entia.*
³⁴ *Metaphysics* 998b 22.
³⁵ "When things have only a name in common and the definition of being which
corresponds to the name is different, they are called homonymous." *Categories* 1a 1.
"When things have the name in common and the definition of being which corresponds
to the name is the same, they are called synonymous." *Categories* 1a 6. J. L. Ackrill, p. 3.
Boethius translates *aequivoce* for homonymously and *univoce* for synonymously. Elias
states. "Now being (τὸ ὄν) is not divided (διαιρεῖται) like a homonymous sound, as
Aristotle said in the *Categories* and now Porphyry, and not like a genus into species, as
Plato said, but ὡς τὰ ἀφ᾽ ἑνὸς καὶ πρὸς ἕν" (p. 70, 18-21). The commentators regularly
explain the Aristotelian position as involving pure equivocity, as Boethius, "that is, as a
sound signifying many things." E.S. p. 223, 23-24.
³⁶ Since the universe is without temporal limit. See Ammonius, p. 85, 2; p. 86, 27-28;
E.P. p. 77.

15 from the highest genera to the lowest spec*ies* and to stop, to
    descend through the intermediary spec*ies* and to divide by
    specific differences. He says to leave the infinite individuals
    alone, for there can be no knowledge of them.[37]

    Thus, in descending to the lowest spec*ies* we must divide and
    traverse a multiplicity, but in ascending to the highest genera we
    must collect together the multiplicity into unity;[q] for the species,
    and still more the genus, is a uniting of the many into one
20 nature.[38] Particulars and singulars, on the other hand, always
    divide unity into multiplicity; for by sharing in the species many
    men are one, but man, one and common, is multiple because of
    particular men. The singular is always divisive, while the com-
    mon is collective and unifying.

    An account has been given of the nature of species and genus,
P. 7 in which genus is one while spec*ies* are many (for the genus is
    always divided into many spec*ies*). The genus is always
    predicated of the species and all the higher of the lower, but the
    species is predicated neither of its own proximate genus nor of
    the higher ones. There is no convertibility of genus and species,
5   for equals must be predicated of equals, as neighing of horse, or
    the greater of the lesser, as animal of man, but never the lesser
    of the greater. You may never say that animal is a man, as you
    may say man is an animal. Necessarily, too, the genus of the
    species and the genus of the genus up to the highest genus will
10 be predicated of whatever things the species is predicated. If it is
    true to say that Socrates is a man, that man is an animal, and

---

q B omits εἰς ἕν.

[37] *Philebus* 16c 5-18d 2. Ammonius cites the *Sophist*, and Busse suggests 266 a-b
and *Politicus* 262 a-c.
[38] εἰς μίαν φύσιν.

that animal is a substance, then it is also true to say that Socrates is an animal and a substance.

Since, therefore, the higher is always predicated of the lower, (1) the species will be predicated of the individual, (2) the genus both of the species and of the individual, and (3) the highest genus of the genus or genera (if there be very many subordinate intermediates), of the species, and of the individual. The highest genus is predicated of all the subordinate genera, spec*ies*, and individuals; the genus prior to the lowest species of all the lowest spec*ies* and individuals; the species alone of all the individuals; but the individual term of one only of the particulars. Socrates, this white, and this approaching son of Sophroniscus, if Socrates be his only son, are called individual. Such things are called individuals because each thing is composed of a collection of characteristics which can never be the same for another; for the characteristics of Socrates could not be the same for any other particular man.[r] The characteristics of man, however, I mean the man in common, will be the same for a great many, more strongly, for *all* particular men as men. Thus, the individual is contained by the species and the species by the genus, for the genus is a kind of whole, the individual a part.[39] The species is both a whole and a part, a part of another and a whole, not of another but in others. The whole is in the parts.

We have now answered these questions about genus and species: (1) what is the highest genus? (2) what is the lowest species? (3) which genera and spec*ies* are the same? (4) what are individuals? and (5) how many ways can we speak of genus and species?

15

20

25

P. 8

5

[r] αἱ γὰρ Σωχράτους ἰδιότητες οὐχ ἂν ἐπ' ἄλλου τινὸς τῶν χατὰ μέρος γένοιντο ἂν αἱ αὐταί Β: *Socratis enim proprietates numquam in alio quolibet erunt particularium.*

[39] "The individual is always a part, never a whole." E.P. p. 82, 16-17. A classic statement of the metaphysical thrust of Platonism and a bit stronger than Porphyry's text.

DIFFERENCE

Let us say that difference has (1) a common meaning, (2) a
proper meaning, and (3) a strict meaning. *Commonly* one thing
is said to differ from another when by otherness it differs in any
10   way at all either from itself or from another, for by otherness
Socrates differs from Plato and, indeed, from himself: he was a
child and became a man;[40] he is doing something or he has
stopped; and, of course, he is always changing in qualitative
degree.[24s] *Properly* two things are said to differ whenever they
differ because of an inseparable accident, such as greyness of the
15   eyes[t] or a hooked quality of the nose or even a scar which has
become hardened from a wound. *Strictly* two things are said to
differ whenever they differ because of a specific difference, as a
man differs from a horse because of a specific difference, the
quality rational.

In general, therefore, every difference added to something
modifies it. But common and proper differences make something
different-in-quality [*alloion*], while strict differences make
20   something different-in-essence [*allo*], for some differences are
qualitative, some are essential. Differences, then, which make
another essence [*allo*] are called specific differences, while those
that produce differences in quality are simply called differences.
P. 9   The difference "rational" added to animal makes another-

per se differences make something different in essence

˅ καὶ ἀεί γε ἐν ταῖς τοῦ πῶς ἔχειν ἑτερότησιν B: *et semper in aliquo modo habendi
alteritatibus.* P: *semperque in varietatibus, quibus est aliquo modo affectus est, cernitur.*
ͭ γλαυχότης B: *caecitas oculorum* P: *oculorum caesius color.*

[40] This became a commonplace. Boethius, Migne PL Vol. 64, 241 D4. Duns Scotus,
Q. XXIV, "Is this true: The old man Socrates differs from himself as a boy?"

essence [*allo*],[u] but the difference "moving" only makes something qualitatively different from resting, so that the one makes a difference-in-essence, the other only a difference-in-quality.

Thus, from essential differences (1) the divisions of genera into spec*ies* arise and (2) definitions are expressed, since they are composed of a genus and such differences; but from qualitative differences common and proper differences[v] and changes in qualitative degree take place.[24]   5

We must begin again from what has been said and say that there are separable and inseparable differences. Moving, resting, being healthy, being ill, and characteristics similar to these are separable, but being hook-nosed, snub-nosed, rational, or irrational are inseparable. Some inseparable differences exist *per se*, some accidentally. Rational, mortal, and being capable of knowledge belong to man *per se*, but hook-nosed or snub-nosed belong accidentally and not *per se*. Differences present *per se*, then, are comprehended in the definition of the substance and make another essence, but accidental differences are not comprehended[w] in the definition of the substance and do not make another essence but only a difference in quality.   15

Differences *per se* do not permit a more or a less, but accidental differences do; and if they are inseparable and accidental, they include increase and decrease.[41] The genus is

---

[u] B adds *et speciem animalis fecit.*
[v] αἱ ἑτερότητες B: *alteratio.*
[w] λαμβάνονται ALG: παραλαμβάνονται B: *dicuntur.*

[41] Ἐπίτασις (tightening) and ἄνεσις (relaxing) seem equivalent to increase and decrease, parallel to "more or less" a line earlier. See E. Zeller, n. 1, p. 103. Also Ammonius, p. 98, 1-7. Elias remarks, however, that an enmattered specific difference does admit of more or less (p. 80, 22-28). Boethius explains, "And so, then, property and dif-

predicated neither more nor less of whatever it is a genus nor are
the differences of the genus by which a genus is divided. These
20 differences complete the definition of each thing. The being of
each thing[42] is one and the same and permits neither increase
nor decrease, while being hook-nosed or snub-nosed or colored
in a particular way is both increased and decreased.

Three species of difference have been observed: (1) the
25 separable and (2) the inseparable, and of the latter (2a) the in-
P. 10 separable *per se* and (2b) the inseparable by accident. We should
also say that among differences *per se* there are some by which
we divide genera into species and some by which the divided
genera are constituted as species. For example, although there
are all the *per se* differences of animal such as animate and sensible, rational and irrational, mortal and immortal, the difference
5 animate and sensible is constitutive of the substance of animal,
for animal is an animate, sensible substance; but the differences
mortal and immortal and that of rational and irrational *divide*
animal, for by these we divide genera into species. These
dividing differences, however, complete the genera and become
10 constitutive of the species, for animal is divided both by the dif-

ference never leave those objects in which they reside. Man is always capable of laughing,
even though he may not laugh; man is always a biped, even though he may have lost a
foot. For, as has been said, in the case of differences and properties we pay attention to
what can exist potentially, not what exists actually." E.P. 122, 19-24. Although two-
footed is a property of the second class (Is under property), it is also classifiable as a *per
se* difference and is frequently used as an example of a difference which can be potential
or *per naturam* in some way. I found no Latin commentator who treated rational in this
way. Boethius adds, "for in substance no man is more or less rational than another
man." E.P. pp. 124-125. "The being (*esse*) of each single thing can neither increase nor
diminish, for no man can sustain an increase or a decrease in his humanity." E.S. p. 252.
8-10.
    [42] Τὸ εἶναι ἑκάστῳ, B: *esse unicuique*. Simplicius says, *Ad Physicam* 174, CAG Vol.
IX, p. 735, δῆλον δὲ ὅτι ἄλλο τοῦτό ἐστι τὸ εἶναι παρ᾽ ἐκεῖνο τὸ συνήθως ὑπὸ τοῦ περιπάτου
λεγόμενον καὶ τὸ εἶδος σημαῖνον. Cited in Bonitz, p. 221, εἶναι 5. See J. Owens, p. 181, n.
83a.

ference of rational and irrational, and again by the difference of mortal and immortal. The differences mortal and rational become constitutive of man, those of rational and immortal of god,[43] those of irrational and mortal of irrational animals. Since the differences animate and inanimate and that of sensible and insensible divide the highest substance, animate and sensible, combined with substance, complete animal, while animate and insensible complete plant.[x] Since, therefore, the same differences understood in one way become constitutive and in another way become divisive, they are all called specific. These differences are especially useful both for the divisions of genera and for definitions, but inseparable accidental differences and, still more, separable differences are *not* useful for this purpose.

[x] ἡ δὲ ἔμψυχος καὶ ἀναίσθητος ἀπετέλεσαν τὸ φύτον B omits.

[43] "Again, some raise this problem: if God is under rational, rational under animal, animal under ensouled, ensouled under body, God will be found under body. We reply that it is not unreasonable for God to be a body, for according to Aristotle heavenly things are gods because they are always 'running' and moving. Nonetheless, the difficulty remains. For, what could one say about God, the first cause? Is he rational or not? We reply that God is rational, but a rational which is not classified under animal. the incomplete, which needs premises and conclusions and, consequently, is composite, but rational as if under reason. For in the same way the rational we apply to soul is not classified under animal but under reason (for, if the soul is under animal and under ensouled, the soul will be found to be ensouled)." Elias, p. 66, 2-12. Boethius says, "for if you place mortal under rational, you will make men; if immortal, you will make God, but a corporeal God; for the ancients used to call this world a god (and they thought a fitting name for him was Jupiter). They also used to call the sun a god as well as the rest of the celestial bodies, which Plato and a whole troop of widely educated men thought were alive." E.S. pp. 208-209, 21-23. Also E.S. p. 293, 15-18. Maurus comments, "... as rational and irrational constitute the spec*ies* of man and God according to the error of the Platonists, who thought the gods, that is angels, were rational, immortal animals; ..." (p. 15). On the Platonic error, "... rational animal is a species of animal and, according to the error of the Platonists, the genus of man; man, according to the same error, is a species of rational animal. Rational animal, however, is not a genus but only a species predicable of singular men who do not differ in species but in number alone; ..." (pp. 10-11). For the problems involved in conjoining immortal and irrational: E.S. pp. 256-258.

Our predecessors also give this definition: difference is that by
P. 11 which the species exceeds the genus. Man, for example,
possesses more than animal, namely the rational and the mortal.
Now animal is none of these, for, if not, how could the spec*ies*
be different from one another? Nor does animal possess all the
contradictory differences, for the same thing at the same time
would have contradictory characteristics. They maintain,
however, that animal possesses potentially, not actually, all the
5   differences of the subordinate spec*ies*.[y] Nothing then arises from
not-being,[44] nor will contradictories exist at the same time[z] in
the same thing.[45]

They also define difference as follows: difference is that
predicated qualitatively of many things which differ in species.
For man is said to be rational and mortal, which are predicated
10   of man qualitatively but not essentially. When we are asked,
"What is man?" it is proper to say, "An animal," but if we
have learned what sort of an animal, we shall define him
properly as rational and mortal. Since things are composed of
matter and form or possess a constitution analogous to matter
and form (as a statue is made of matter and form, the copper
15   and the shape), so too, the common and formal man is composed of something analogous to matter and to shape, the genus

[y] τὰς τῶν ὑφ᾽ αὑτὸ διαφοράς ALG: τῶν ὑπ᾽ αὑτό B: *sub se differentias.*
[z] B omits ἅμα P: *simul.*

[44] ἐξ οὐκ ὄντων. Since the characteristics are contained potentially in the genus, they
are not nothing.
[45] Ammonius states the difficulty which Porphyry is trying to remove: "If the differences exist in the genera, opposites will exist in the same thing at the same time, as
mortal and immortal, rational and irrational. This is impossible. If differences do not
exist in the genera, from what source do they arise in the species?" (p. 101, 17-19).
Also, George Berkeley's *Principles of Human Knowledge,* Introduction, Section 6ff. Consult A. C. Lloyd's "Neoplatonic Logic and Aristotelian Logic," pp. 153-154.

and the difference. This whole, rational-mortal-animal, is man, in a way similar to the statue mentioned above.

They also indicate such differences as follows: difference is what naturally separates the spec*ies* under the same genus, for   20 rational and irrational separate man and horse which are under the same genus, animal.

They also give this definition: difference is that by which singulars differ.[a] Man and horse[b] do not differ in genus, for we are mortal animals and also irrational; but rational, when added, distinguishes us from them. Also, both the gods and ourselves are rational, but mortal, when added, distinguishes us from   P. 12 them. In working out further the meaning of difference they state that the difference is not any chance characteristic which divides the species under the same genus but what contributes to the being[42] and what is part of the essence[46] of the thing. The natural inclination to sail is not a difference of man, even if it is a property of his.   5

We would say that some animals have a natural tendency to sail, others do not, and we would divide one group from the other. The natural tendency to sail, however, does not complete the substance nor is it a part of it; rather, it is only an inclination in conformity with the substance,[c] because it is not the sort of difference which is called properly specific.

Specific differences, therefore, will be those which make a species different and which are comprehended in the essence.[46]   10
This is a sufficient description of difference.

[a] B adds *a se.*
[b] B omits ἄνθρωπος γὰρ καὶ ἵππος.
[c] ἐπιτηδειότης μόνον αὐτῆς B: *aptitudo quaedam eius.*

[46] Τὸ τί ἦν εἶναι. This difficult Aristotelian expression occurs only twice in the *Isagoge.* For a detailed discussion of its meaning see J. Owens, pp. 181-188. *Topics* 101b 6, ἔστι δ᾽ ὅρος μὲν λόγος ὁ τὸ τί ἦν εἶναι σημαίνων, repeated by Boethius, *Si quis quod est esse monstrare voluerit, definitionem dicit.* E.S. 273, 14-15. Boethius has *quod est esse* in the first occurrence and *quod quale est* in the second. P: *quidditas.*

PROPERTY

Our predecessors distinguish four meanings of property: (1)
what occurs in one species only, although not in every member
of the species, as healing and measuring occur in man; (2) what
occurs in the entire species and not in it only, as being two-
15   footed occurs in man; (3) what occurs in the entire species, in it
only, and at some time, as becoming grey in old age occurs in
every man; and (4) what occurs in the entire species, in it only,
and always, as the capacity to laugh in man. For even if a man
does not always laugh, still he is said to be capable of laughing,
not because he is always laughing but because it is natural for
him to laugh. This characteristic always belongs to a man
20   naturally as the capacity to neigh belongs to a horse. They say,
too, that these characteristics are properties in the strict sense,
because they are also convertible. For if [d] there is a horse, there
is the capacity to neigh, and if [d] there is the capacity to neigh,
there is a horse.

ACCIDENT

What comes into being and passes away apart from the
25   destruction of the substratum[47] is an accident. Two types are
distinguished, the separable and the inseparable. Sleeping is a

---

[d] B: *quicquid.*

[47] 'Υποχειμένου, B: *subiecti.* Some might prefer "subject." The more general term,
substratum, seems better, for it shows a linguistic and philosophical link between the
categories and Aristotle's physics and metaphysics. Substratum may refer to the material
which is qualified by the presence of a characteristic, as a few lines below, as well as to
the subject of predication.

separable accident, while being black occurs inseparably in the crow and in the Ethiopian. It is possible, however, to conceive of a white crow and of an Ethiopian who has lost his color apart from the destruction of the substratum.[48]

P. 13

They also give this definition: accident is what can belong or not belong to the same thing,[e] or what is neither a genus, nor a difference, nor a species, nor a property, but always exists in a substratum.[49]

5

Since all the terms put forward have been defined — I mean genus, species, difference, property, and accident — we must state those characteristics common to all and those peculiar to each.

COMMON CHARACTERISTICS OF THE FIVE PREDICABLES

All the predicables are predicated of many things. The genus is predicated of spec*ies* and individuals, and the difference in the same way, but the species is predicated of the individuals under

10

---

[e] ὃ ἐνδέχεται τῷ αὐτῷ ὑπάρχειν ἢ μὴ ὑπάρχειν B: *quod contingit eidem esse et non esse.*

[48] Pacius, *Analyticus Commentarius,* pp. 17-18, sums up the following distinctions: (a) difference signifies the form and essence of a thing but cannot be removed from the thing itself or be considered as separate by the intellect; (b) a separable accident can be removed from the thing and considered as separate by the intellect, while an inseparable accident can be considered apart by the intellect but not removed from the thing; and (c) property is the median between difference and separable accident, namely an accident which flows from the form. It cannot be removed from the thing but can be considered in the intellect as removed. Boethius remarks, "... not because Ethiopian and crow lose color, but because without that color they can subsist for our understanding." E.P. p. 101, 1-3.

[49] Although Maurus prints the translation of Pacius *semper autem in subjecto inhaeret,* in his commentary he repeats verbatim the translation of Boethius *semper autem est in subjecto subsistens.*

it; the property of its species and of the individuals under the species; and the accident of spec*ies* and individuals. Animal, for example, is predicated of the spec*ies* horse and ox,[f] and of the
15 individuals "this horse" and "this ox," while irrational is predicated of the spec*ies* horse and ox and of particulars. A species, such as man, is predicated only of particulars, while a property, as the capacity to laugh, is predicated both of man and of particulars. Black, an inseparable accident, is predicated of the species crow and of particulars; and moving, a separable ac-
20 cident, of man and of horse. Moving, however, is predicated primarily of individuals, secondarily of the spec*ies* which contain the individuals.

COMMON CHARACTERISTICS OF GENUS
AND DIFFERENCE

Both genus and difference contain spec*ies*, for the difference,
P. 14 too, contains spec*ies*, even though not all that the genera contain. Rational, for example, although it does not contain irrational things as animal does,[g] still contains man and god, which are spec*ies*. Whatever is predicated of the genus as genus is predicated also of the spec*ies* under it; and whatever is predicated of the difference as difference will also be predicated
5 of the species formed from it. For example, substance and animate are predicated of the genus animal as genus, but also they are predicated of all the spec*ies* under animal even down to individuals. Since rational is a difference, using reason is predicated of a difference, but using reason will be predicated not only of rational but also of the spec*ies* under rational.

---

[f] B adds *et canibus*, omits εἰδῶν ὄντων.
[g] τὸ γὰρ λογικὸν εἰ καὶ μὴ περιέχει τὰ ἄλογα ὥσπερ τὸ ζῶον B: *rationale enim etiam si non continet ea quae sunt inrationabilia, ut genus, quemadmodum animal.*

There is another common characteristic. If the genus or dif-   10
ference is destroyed, the things under them are destroyed; for if
animal does not exist, neither horse nor man exists. In the same
way, if rational does not exist, the animal which uses reason will
not exist.

THE DIFFERENCE BETWEEN GENUS
AND DIFFERENCE

It is a property of the genus to be predicated of more things
than the difference, the species, the property, and the accident.   15
Animal is predicated of man, horse, bird, and serpent, but four-
footed is predicated only of those creatures which have four feet,
man of individuals only, the capacity to neigh only [h] of horse
and of particular horses, and an accident likewise of fewer
things. Here we must understand as differences those which
divide the genus, not those which complete the substance of the   20
genus. Further, the genus contains the difference potentially, for
the differences of animal are rational and irrational.

Genera are prior to the differences under themselves, because
they destroy the differences but are not themselves destroyed. If,
for example, animal is destroyed, rational and irrational are   P. 15
destroyed, but differences never destroy the genus, for even if all
differences are removed, animate sensible substance, which is
animal, is conceivable.[i] Further, as has been said, genus is
predicated essentially, but difference qualitatively. Another
point: there is one genus for each species, as animal for man, but
there are many differences, as rational, mortal, and capable of   5

---

[h] B omits μόνον.
[i] ἐπινοεῖται B: subintellegi potest. The terms suggest "conceivable in thought," even if
the object does not exist as conceived.

understanding and knowledge which distinguish man from other animals. Finally the genus is like matter, but the difference like form.

Although we could add other characteristics common and unique to the genus and the difference, let this discussion suffice.

Common Characteristics of Genus and Species

10   As has been said genus and species are predicated of many things. In this discussion let the species be understood as species only and not as genus as well, if the same class is both species and genus. Genus and species also have in common that both are prior to the things of which they are predicated and that each is a kind of whole.

The Difference Between Genus and Species

15   They differ insofar as the genus contains spec*ies* ʲ and spec*ies* do not contain genera but are contained, for the genus is more extensive than the species. Further, genera must be admitted beforehand and, when informed by the specific differences, complete the species. For the same reason genera are naturally prior to spec*ies*. Also, the genera destroy the spec*ies* but are not
20   destroyed. If there is a species, there assuredly exists a genus also, but if there is a genus, the existence of the species is not also assured. Genera are predicated synonymously of their subordinate ᵏ spec*ies* but spec*ies* are never predicated of genera.

ʲ B adds *sub se*.
ᵏ B omits ὑφ' ἑαυτά.

In addition genera have more by containing their subordinate *species*, while *species* in their proper differences have more than their genera. Further, a species can not become a highest genus nor can a genus become a lowest species.

COMMON CHARACTERISTICS OF GENUS   P. 16

AND PROPERTY

Genus and property are consequences of the spe*cies*. If there is man, there is animal, and if there is man, there is the capacity to laugh. Also, the genus is predicated equally of its spe*cies* and the property equally of the individuals[1] who share in it, for man and ox are equally animal and Anytus and Meletus are equally   5 capable of laughter. They have in common, as well, that they are predicated synonymously: the genus of the proper spe*cies* and the property of whatever it belongs to.

THE DIFFERENCE BETWEEN GENUS AND PROPERTY

They differ because genus is prior and property posterior. There must be animal; next it must be divided by differences and properties. The genus is predicated of many spe*cies* but the   10 property of the one species to which it belongs. The property is predicated convertibly with its species, while the genus is convertible with nothing. For example, it is neither the case that if there is animal, there is man, nor that if there is animal, there is the capacity to laugh; but, if there is man, there is the capacity to laugh and *vice versa*.

The property belongs always and only to all of its species.   15 The genus, however, belongs always but not only to all its

---

[1] B omits ἀτόμων.

species. In addition properties, if destroyed, do not destroy the genera, but genera, if destroyed, destroy the species which the properties belong to.ᵐ Consequently, if the species which the properties belong to are destroyed, then, too, the properties themselves are destroyed.

COMMON CHARACTERISTICS OF GENUS AND ACCIDENT

20   As has been said, genus and accident are predicated of many things, whether the accidents are separable or inseparable. For
P. 17 example, moving is predicated of many things, and black is predicated of crows, Ethiopians, and some inanimate things.

THE DIFFERENCE BETWEEN GENUS AND ACCIDENT

Genus differs from accident because in relation to species the genus is prior while accidents are posterior. For, although an ac-
5   cident is understood as inseparable, still what an accident belongs to is prior to the accident. Also, things share equally in the genus but unequally in the accident, for sharing in accidents permits increase and decrease, while sharing in genera never does. Accidents exist principally in individuals, but genera and
10   species are naturally prior to individual substances.⁵⁰ Also,

---

ᵐ ἔτι τὰ μὲν ἴδια ἀναιρούμενα οὐ συναιρεῖ τὰ γένη, τὰ δὲ γένη ἀναιρούμενα συναιρεῖ τὰ εἴδη, ὧν ἐστιν ἴδια B: amplius species quidem interemptae non simul interimunt genera, propria vero interempta simul interimunt, quorum sunt propria.

---

⁵⁰ Maurus remarks, "... Porphyry seems to say this in agreement with Plato who puts the Ideas before singular things" (p. 22, § 28). Yet presumably Maurus does not regard the priority of genus to species and the rest in the formula "If the genus were to be removed, all things under it would be removed" as Platonic, because the latter is a

genera are predicated essentially of their subordinates, but accidents qualitatively or in some degree of quality.[24] If, for example, you are asked, "What sort of man is an Ethiopian?" you will say, "Black"; and if you are asked, "What position is Socrates in?"[24] you will say that he is sitting or that he is walking.

We have now discussed how the genus differs from the other four predicables, but in addition each predicable differs from the four others. Since there are five predicables all together and each one differs from the other four, then if five is multiplied by four, the total number of differences becomes twenty. But this is not accurate.[n] When items in a series are counted in order, the two's always have one difference less because that difference has already been accounted for; the three's, two less; the four's, three less; and the five's, four less. The total number of differences becomes ten: four plus three plus two plus one. For example, the genus differs from the difference, the species, the property, and the accident. There are, therefore, four differences. We have already said how the difference differs from the genus when we

15

20

[n] B omits.

distinction of conceptual priority which does not necessarily involve existence. I think that this is a questionable point of view, given the metaphysical presuppositions inherent in the whole scheme of the predicables. "But it can be said that we come upon genera as well as species after individual things; for, unless there are single men and single horses, the species 'man' and 'horse' cannot exist; and if singular species do not exist, the genus of these, animal, will not exist. But we ought to remember what was said above, that genus does not constitute its substance from the things which it is predicated of, but rather genus is completed in substance and form by constitutive differences." E.S. p. 316, 7-14. Ockham, however, says, "We ought to understand first that the author is not thinking of a destruction ... of any real thing; for, since neither genus nor species exists except as some mental intention or concept, it is possible that that intention which is a genus may be destroyed in the soul while that intention which is a species remains in the soul; ..." *Expositio In Librum Porphyrii De Praedicabilibus*, Gulielmi Ockham, edidit E. A. Moody, Franciscan Institute, St. Bonaventure, N. Y., 1965, p. 108, 7-13.

say how the genus differs from the difference. It will remain for
us to say how the difference differs from the species, the
25   property, and the accident. The number of differences becomes
three. In turn, we said how the species differs from the difference
P. 18 when we said how the difference differs from the species. We
said how the species differs from the genus when we said how
the genus differs from the species. Thus, it will remain for us to
say how the species differs from the property and the accident.
These differences are two. There will remain the explanation of
how the property differs from the accident. For how the property
differs from the species, the difference, and the genus was men-
5   tioned earlier in their differences from it. Since, therefore, we
understand four differences of the genus from the others, three
of the difference, two of the species, and one of the property
from the accident, the total number of differences will be ten,
four of which we explained earlier as differences of the genus
from the other predicables.

10   COMMON CHARACTERISTICS OF DIFFERENCE
                      AND SPECIES

Difference and species are shared equally, for particular men
share equally in man and the difference rational. Also they both
are always present to things that share in them, for Socrates is
always rational and always a man.

15   THE DIFFERENCE BETWEEN SPECIES AND DIFFERENCE

It is a property of difference to be predicated qualitatively but
a property of species to be predicated essentially. For if man is
understood qualitatively, the quality is not quality simply but
quality insofar as differences are added to the genus and con-

stitute the species. The difference, too, is often observed in many species, as four-footed in a great many animals which differ in   20 species, while the species exists only in the individuals under the species. In addition, the difference is prior to the species formed by it; for rational, if destroyed, destroys man, but man, if destroyed, does not destroy rational, since there is god. Again, difference is joined with another difference, for rational and mortal are joined to form the substance[51] of man, but species is   P. 19 not joined to species to bring forth some other species. A horse, for example, copulates with an ass to produce a mule, but horse simply joined to ass could not produce mule.

COMMON CHARACTERISTICS OF DIFFERENCE AND PROPERTY

Difference and property are shared equally by things that   5 share in them, for rational beings are equally rational and beings capable of laughing are equally capable of laughing. Both are present always and to every member of the species, for even if a two-footed man is maimed,[o] two-footed is always predicated of him due to his natural tendency, so he also always possesses the capacity to laugh because it is natural for him, not because he is always laughing.[52]

---

[o] B adds *non substantiam perimit.*

[51] 'Υπόστασιν, B: *substantia.* This Greek term occurs only once in this text. In all other cases "substance" translates οὐσία. For the force of the term see n. 11.

[52] As is well known the relations between difference, property, and accident were subject to ambiguity and confusion. Properties are classified as *per se* differences and so are comprehended in the definition (Is p. 9, 11 ff.) and are predicated equally (Is 16, 2 ff.) but can be classified as accidents (E.S. p. 276, 3-11). Differences, too, are classified in various ways. In the passage before us the ambiguity turns on the distinction between a *per se* difference, bipedality, which is also designated a property, and a specific difference, rationality. Maurus remarks, "Secondly, they agree in that they belong to the entire

10   THE DIFFERENCE BETWEEN PROPERTY AND DIFFERENCE

It is a property of difference that it is often predicated of many spec*ies*, as rational is predicated of god and man, but property is predicated of the single species it belongs to. Difference is a consequence of those things whose difference it is,

species, to it only, and always. For just as every man is always rational, so also every man is always capable of laughing. In order to avoid ambiguity Porphyry observes that properties and differences ought to be affirmed as natural tendencies, not as actual facts. For example, it is not a difference of man to have *in fact* two feet, for a man can actually have one foot because his other foot has been cut off. The difference of man is to tend, from his own nature, to have two feet. In like manner it is a property of man in the fourth sense not to be actually laughing but from his own nature to tend to laugh'' (p. 23, 36). See also E.P. p. 122 and E.S. pp. 325-326, and n. 45. To hold that all men are equally rational is not necessarily to claim that all men actually think equally well but that they all have the inborn tendency (a) to think and perhaps (b) to think equally well. The weight of the doctrine falls on an interpretation of potentiality. There are two steps, at least, in the understanding of this potentiality: (1) since Socrates and Euthyphro are both engaged in thinking, one predicates thinking equally of them both. The presence of the quality allows for univocal predication. (2) Since Socrates thinks well and Euthyphro thinks badly, one cannot predicate univocally except in terms of the perfected goal. Boethius would say, I think, that we are speaking of the singular and not of substance. E.S. p. 331, 8-9. Thinking *in actu* is present to both in varying degrees. *The first case* seems to be the model for Porphyry and to a great extent Boethius though they modify their views with a doctrine of potentiality or natural tendency for difference and property. The example used by Boethius and Maurus to show the potentiality of difference is bipedality, not rationality, and it is tempting to suppose that the example is chosen because a numerical property like twoness cannot be shared in degrees, so one is either actually or potentially two-footed. In affirming the equal-predication doctrine they use rational, and in affirming the potentiality of difference, two-footed. *The second case* arises if one wishes to claim that, although men do not *actually* think equally well, they all *could* if they tried. That some philosophers thought so is well known. The doctrine, however, does not require that view. All men have the same essence as a goal, τὸ τί ἦν εἶναι, but εἶδος as existing in a given man at a given time only partially shares the qualitative fullness of the essence. All men may not be equally apt to reach the goal. In discussing property Boethius remarks, ''Cato and Cicero are equally capable of laughing, although they do not laugh equally; for to the extent that they tend to laugh and not because they may now be laughing, they can be called 'able' to laugh.'' E.S. p. 309, 2-5. But, with this admission, how can one claim that difference differs from accident in not admitting more or less, since in a sense it does? The answer lies in the notion that an acbut it is not also convertible with them. Properties, however, are predicated reciprocally of whatever things they are the properties, because things and their properties are convertible. 15

COMMON CHARACTERISTICS OF DIFFERENCE AND ACCIDENT

Difference and accident are predicated of many things, but inseparable accidents and difference are also present always and to every member of the species, for two-footed is always present to all crows, and black in the same way.

PROPERTIES OF DIFFERENCE AND ACCIDENT 20

They differ because the difference contains rather than is contained, for rational contains man. Yet, in one way accidents contain because they exist in many things, while in another they are contained because the substrata are not receptive of one accident P. 20

---

cident is not connected to the essence as a natural tendency, and, therefore, is predicated *primarily* to the degree that it actually exists in a singular. The difference, however, is predicated in terms of the essence as fulfilled in the attainment of the end, τὸ τέλος or τὸ τί ἦν εἶναι. Thus, genus, species, difference, and property can be predicated univocally in terms of the end as the completed goal. Thus, in addition to the potentiality (and total actualization) discussed by Porphyry and Boethius, one can raise the possibility of partial actualization and degrees of fulfillment. Boethius interprets the doctrine of "equal predication" in terms of Platonic participation, and there is no question that this is the issue: how to properly understand Aristotle's theory of predication such that it allows for some form of participation. Univocal predication means equal sharing; equivocal predication means no sharing; while analogical predication means unequal sharing. Porphyry, in his discussion of accidents, allows for more or less, intension and remission, but equal participation in genera, species, specific differences, and properties. He allows for some potentiality in differences and in properties, though differences and properties *in actu* are equal for each singular; i.e., all two-footed men are equally so, as all men who laugh laugh equally. Potentiality does not imply the *partial* fulfillment which can occur in the doctrine of Platonic participation.

but of many. In addition, the difference is not increased or
decreased, but accidents permit a more and a less. Opposite dif-
5   ferences do not mix, but opposite accidents may mix.

Such, therefore, are the characteristics, common and unique,
of difference and the other predicables. We explained how the
species differs from genus and difference in showing how genus
10   and difference differ from the others.

COMMON CHARACTERISTICS OF SPECIES AND PROPERTY

Species and property are predicated reciprocally of each other.
For if there is man, there is the capacity to laugh; and if there is
the capacity to laugh, there is man. It has often been said that
admittedly our capacity to laugh arises from our natural tendency to laugh, for the spec*ies* are present equally to those that
15   share in them and the properties equally to those things they
belong to.

THE DIFFERENCE BETWEEN SPECIES AND PROPERTY

The species differs from the property because it is able to be a
genus of others, but it is impossible for the property to be a
property of others. The species, too, is constituted before the
property, while the property comes into being after the species,
20   for there must be man for there to be the capacity to laugh. Further, the species always is actually present to the substratum,
while the property sometimes is present potentially. Socrates is
always actually a man, but he does not always laugh, although it
is always natural for him to laugh. Again, those things differ
P. 21   whose definitions differ. The species is defined as (1) that under

the genus, (2) that predicated essentially of many things which differ in number, and (3) other characteristics such as these, but the property is defined as that present always and only to the entire species.

COMMON CHARACTERISTICS OF SPECIES AND ACCIDENT

Species and accident are predicated of many things, but the   5
other common characteristics are rare because the accident and what it belongs to are widely separated from each other.

THE DIFFERENCE BETWEEN SPECIES AND ACCIDENT

Each has its properties: the species is predicated essentially of those things it belongs to; the accident is predicated qualitatively   10
or in some degree of quality.[24] Also, each substance shares in one species but in many accidents, both separable and inseparable. The species, in addition, are conceived before the accidents, even if they are inseparable (for there must be the substratum in order that something be an accident of the substratum), but accidents naturally exist later and possess an ad-   15
ventitious nature. Further, the sharing in the species is equal, while sharing in the accident, even if inseparable, is not equal; for one Ethiopian, more than another, may have his color either intensified or reduced in blackness.

It remains finally to speak about property and accident, for we have discussed how the property differs from the species, the difference, and the genus.

20   COMMON CHARACTERISTICS OF PROPERTY AND
                    THE INSEPARABLE ACCIDENT

P. 22
It is a common characteristic of the property and the inseparable accident that those things in which they are observed
do not exist without them, for as man does not exist without the
capacity to laugh, so neither can an Ethiopian exist without
being black. And, as the property is always present to every
member of the species, so also is the inseparable accident.

        THE DIFFERENCE BETWEEN PROPERTY AND THE
                    INSEPARABLE ACCIDENT

5
They differ because the property is present to one species
only, as the capacity to laugh is present to man, but the inseparable accident, such as black, is present not only to the
Ethiopian but also to the crow, to charcoal, to ebony, and to
some others. Thus, the property is predicated equally and convertibly with what it belongs to, but the inseparable accident is
10   not convertible. Also, the sharing of the properties is equal, that
of the accidents involves a more or a less.

There are also other characteristics of the predicables, some
common and some unique, but these are sufficient for
distinguishing among them and for exhibiting their common
characteristics.

INDEX